CW00796960

The

2023 Long

James Cubby

Cover Photo by Kate Honish from Pixabay

MARTHA'S VINEYARD
The Cubby
Long Weekend Guide

TABLES OF CONTENTS

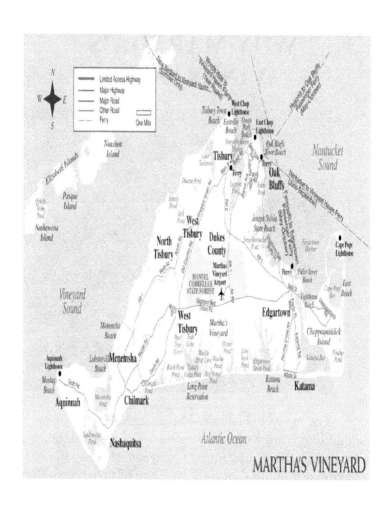

MARTHA'S VINEYARD

Chapter 1
WHY MARTHA'S VINEYARD?

The answer is simple—because there's no place quite like it anywhere in America. Yes, you might find some things in common between islands off Georgia or South Carolina, but none of them carry the same *élan* as Martha's Vineyard. The type of people—dare I say the *quality* of people? —that trek to Martha's Vineyard every summer are without doubt the best of the best. It's a little like Sag Harbor, but more of it.

Here on an island that used to be a whaling center you have what some people call "Hollywood East."

You get celebrities, yes, but also writers and academics and practically the entire East Coast Establishment intelligentsia. Conversation in the restaurants and bars always seems elevated to a fascinating level.

On all those other islands—from Pawleys Island to Catalina—people go to get away from it all. Here on Martha's Vineyard, they bring a little of what they left behind with them.

If you spend enough time here, you'll see what I mean. You just meet the most interesting people in the world.

Whether you agree with their views or not is another matter, but that's why it's fun and stimulating to talk to them.

vineyard vines

Martha's Vineyard is broken up into 6 towns divided into the two sides of the island called Up Island and Down Island. (Though it would be more accurate for these divisions to be East Island and West Island.)

UP ISLAND TOWNS
AQUINNAH. The <u>Gay Head Lighthouse</u> is out here on the western end.

CHILMARK. Still a quaint area with charming fishing villages and boats bobbing in the water.

WEST TISBURY. Wild expanses of empty land. You'll be surprised to see there's so much of it still left. Lots of locals are fierce preservationists.

DOWN ISLAND TOWNS
EDGARTOWN. One of the oldest parts of Martha's Vineyard, here's you'll see beautiful old homes once inhabited by the rich whaling captains.

OAK BLUFFS. Tourist Central, though I hate to put it that way. Lots of 19th Century architectural gems here, numerous shops, eateries.

VINEYARD HAVEN. The big ferry terminus is here in Vineyard Haven. Lots of great little shops.

Chapter 2
GETTING ABOUT

The island is only 7 to 8 miles from Cape Cod, and you can hop a ferry to Martha's Vineyard from Falmouth, Hyannis, Nantucket, New Bedford and Woods Hole in Massachusetts; Quonset Point in Rhode Island, Montauk on Long Island and also New York City.

Ferries from Woods Hole to Martha's Vineyard run year-round. Others run seasonally. Check schedules. Full list can be found at www.mvy.com.

If you're bringing your car, you must use the ferry at Woods Hole. Complete information at www.vineyardferries.com. 508-477-8600. Trip runs 45 minutes.

If you're coming as a passenger from Cape Cod, it runs about an hour from Hyannis on the **Hy-Line,** www.hylinecruises.com. 800-492-8082.
From Falmouth on the **Island Queen** it takes about a half hour: www.islandqueen.com. 508-548-4800.
Once on the island, you can use the pretty efficient bus system that runs all over the place. The Martha's Vineyard Transit Authority, Edgartown, www.vineyardtransit.com - 508-693-9440.

Lots of taxis are also available.

Or you can rent bikes or scooters.

MARTHA'S VINEYARD BIKE RENTALS
One Main St, Edgartown, 800-627-2763
Email: marthas@marthasvineyardbikes.com
www.marthasvineyardbike.com
Pick-up and delivery to any island location.

VINEYARD VEHICLES RENTALS
Beach Rd, Vineyard Haven, 508-693-1185.

Or rent a car or moped from:

A-A ISLAND AUTO RENTAL
800-627-6333, 508-696-5300
info@mvautorental.com
www.mvautorental.com
They have locations in Vineyard Haven, Oak Bluffs
and Edgartown.

Chapter 3
WHERE TO STAY

BEACH PLUM INN
50 Beach Plum Ln, Chilmark, 508-645-9454
www.beachpluminn.com
They only have a dozen rooms in this charming little
inn on a hill overlooking Menemsha Harbor. Superior
views in a wide vista. Lots of bright pastels are used
in the rooms. You'll love the alpacas that live on the
property. Just as attractive is the restaurant here, also
called the **Beach Plum** that has a brief menu that

changes daily. (Cucumber soup, Monkfish liver crostini, lamb burger, roasted chicken for 2.)

CHARLOTTE INN
27 S Summer St, Edgartown, 508-627-4751
www.thecharlotteinn.com
The 20 rooms here look and feel absolutely nothing like what you're used to. Meaning that they don't feel like "hotel" rooms. They look as if you've been given a lavish guest-room in somebody's large private home. The rooms are so beautifully and painstakingly decorated. Grandfather clocks, antiques in every room, plush bedding and comforters, lots of bric-a-brac. (The quality of the furnishings probably accounts for their "no kids under 14" policy, and I don't blame them one bit.) The white clapboard house dates from 1864, and obviously belonged to a rich merchant or a whaling captain. Tall linden trees rise outside. (Those of you who know the place will be aware the restaurant management changes here every now and then, but it's always an elegant place to dine.

Get the lemon pot de crème, the lobster-guacamole starter, blue cheese and fig risotto. Also, they warn you about a strict dress code, but it's not always enforced.

THE DOCKSIDE INN
9 Circuit Ave, Oak Bluffs, 800-245-5979
www.vineyardinns.com
Only 21 rooms in this boutique style property where everything is tastefully elegant. It's just a few feet from the Oak Bluffs ferry terminal, and from their wide wraparound porches, you can see boats making their way in and out of the harbor. They have a 1956 Rolls Royce Silver Cloud they use as a courtesy car.

HARBOR VIEW HOTEL
131 N Water St, Edgartown, 877-624-7992
www.harborviewhotel.com
This historic property went up in 1891, and they still have the rocking chairs on the wide porches to prove it. Great views, personal service, open year-round. I like the rooms in the old main building, but they have

more modern lodgings in their Governor Mayhew Building. They also have cottages and suites in another building. (In fact, they offer such a wide choice of lodgings you'd do well to investigate them all before deciding what to book.) Has an excellent dining room and a very nice bar, **Henry's Hotel Bar**. Again, since they're open around the year, this is a perfect place to spend a romantic weekend—yes, even in the winter.

HOB KNOB

128 Main St, Edgartown, 508-627-9510
www.hobknob.com
Love the name of this charming B&B with its relaxing porches and cozy lobby with a fireplace they use in the winter. (There's a history about the name, but you'll find that out when you get here.) They offer 17 plush rooms, comfortably decorated, and not as "fuddy-duddy" as some of the other, older inns. (They also have 2 houses for rent year-round, the Tilton House and Thaxter House—these houses have kitchens a gourmet would love to work in, so they make good choices if you want to cook.) They're proud to say they are an "eco-lodging," and your breakfast and afternoon tea are made with ingredients supplied by local farms. Business center services, spa treatments, fitness room, sauna & steam. They also have a Boston Whaler you can use to go out to survey the Vineyard from the water—or go fishing.

MARTHA'S VINEYARD RESORT
111 New York Ave, Oak Bluffs, 800-874-4403
NO WEBSITE
Has 6 nice rooms and 2 suites. The rooms are a little
small and somewhat Spartan, but suitable. Very
convenient to everything. Large lobby is great for
meeting other guests or entertaining friends.

WINNETU OCEANSIDE RESORT
31 Dunes Rd, Edgartown, 508-310-1733
www.winnetu.com
The 54-suite Winnetu is as close as the Vineyard gets
to a mega-resort, with a library, fitness center, and
vast lawn outfitted with a nine-hole putting green and
a turtle pond. The hotel is just a 250-yard walk from
the beach.

Chapter 4
WHERE TO EAT

Many restaurants close in the winter off-season and others trim their hours. Check to make sure.

Only 2 towns allow alcohol to be sold: Edgartown and Oak Bluffs. Vineyard Haven has jumped in and now lets restaurants serve beer and wine (but no hard liquor), and then you must have food served as well.

These are odd rules you expect in backwater counties in North Carolina, but not up here. Anyway, in the other towns, West Tisbury, Chilmark and Aquinnah, you must BYOB.

7A FOODS
1045 State Rd, West Tisbury, (508) 693-4636
www.7afoods.com
CUISINE: Breakfast/Sandwiches
DRINKS: No Booze
SERVING: Breakfast & Lunch, Closed Sundays
PRICE RANGE: $$
Take-out spot focusing on breakfast and lunch – fresh baked goods and sandwiches. Order from the blackboard menu on the wall behind the counter. Favorites: Chicken Salad Sandwich and a concoction they call the Liz Lemon (sandwich with pastrami, turkey, Swiss, coleslaw and Russian dressing, very satisfying, I promise). Also, a mini-market offering staples like milk, eggs, and cheese. The sea salt they sell here is made on the island, as are a lot of the jams and other items they have on offer.

ALCHEMY BISTRO & BAR
71 Main St, Edgartown, 508-627-9999
www.alchemyedgartown.com
CUISINE: Seafood, New American
DRINKS: Full bar
SERVING: Dinner
PRICE RANGE: $$$
This classy joint gets loud, but it's FUN. The bar
serves up inventive sophisticated specialty cocktails.
Try the flash fried zucchini matchsticks. Later, go for
the pan-fried halibut with crispy skin or the soft-shell
crabs with a cornmeal breading.

AMONG THE FLOWERS CAFÉ

17 Mayhew Ln, Edgartown, 508-627-3233
https://amongtheflowersmv.com/
CUISINE: American
DRINKS: Beer & Wine Only
SERVING: Breakfast, Lunch, & Dinner
PRICE RANGE: $$
Just a block from the Edgartown harbor is this
popular small café offering a menu of comfort food
standards including delicious sandwiches and salads.
Get a seat in the brick patio where there's plenty of
shade in the summer. Great breakfast pick. Favorites
include Lobster rolls and Turkey & Swiss sandwich.
Gluten-free options available.

ART CLIFF DINER

39 Beach Rd, Vineyard Haven, 508-693-1224
www.artcliffdiner.com
CUISINE: American
DRINKS: No Booze
SERVING: Breakfast, Lunch
PRICE RANGE: $$
Retro diner offering a menu of American classics. It has those old-time swivel stools at the lunch counter, and I've hated them all my life, almost as long as this place has been open, which is decades. But I put up with them because the diner food is so good.

ATLANTIC FISH & CHOP HOUSE

2 Main St, Edgartown, 508-627-7001
www.atlanticmv.com
CUISINE: Seafood
DRINKS: Full Bar
SERVING: Lunch, Dinner
PRICE RANGE: $$$
Casual eatery that feels more like a yacht club (because of its lively bar scene) than a restaurant. Great menu of steaks and seafood. Favorites include Tuna tartare and Lobster roll. Hangout on the second-level deck.

BACK DOOR DONUTS

1-11 Kennebec Ave, Oak Bluffs, 508-693-3688
www.backdoordonuts.com
CUISINE: Bakery
DRINKS: No Booze
SERVING: 7 pm till after midnight in summer. (Has seasonal hours—check first)
PRICE RANGE: $

Nondescript back door in a parking lot attracts long lines when it opens after the sun goes down. Bakery offers an impressive selection of donuts, oversized apple fritters (for which they're famous), cookies, eclairs, cannolis, croissants, fruit squares, fruit turnovers, and scones. All this served out the back door. Note: there's usually a long line waiting. They also serve sandwiches.

BARN BOWL & BISTRO
13 Uncas Ave, Oak Bluffs, 508-696-9800
www.thebarnmv.com
CUISINE: New American (Bowling Alley)
DRINKS: Full bar
SERVING: Lunch & Dinner – year-round
PRICE RANGE: $$
Busy bowling alley (10 regulation lanes) with a bright
and cheery bar and eatery (that while it overlooks the
lanes, is soundproofed so the noise doesn't ruin your
time eating) serving burgers, pizza, and other nibbles.
Favorites: BBQ Chicken Pizza and Fish sandwich.

THE BLACK DOG TAVERN
20 Beach St Extension, Vineyard Haven, 508-693-
9223
www.theblackdog.com
CUISINE: Seafood, American
DRINKS: Beer & Wine Only
SERVING: Breakfast (from 7), Lunch & Dinner

PRICE RANGE: $$

This is quite a place. You'll notice their logo plastered all over the island. The inside is decorated with a wondrous array of nautical artifacts, everything from netting to tackle, buoys, oars—you get the idea. It's just that there's so much of it. Sit outside at a picnic table and take in the splendid waterfront view. You're here for the view. Service is spotty and the food is OK, most especially the lobster mac & cheese, the chowders, the egg dishes in the morning.

COPPER WOK
9, Main St, Vineyard Haven, 508-693-3416
www.copperwokmv.com
CUISINE: Sushi/Japanese
DRINKS: Full bar
SERVING: Lunch & Dinner
PRICE RANGE: $$
Modern eatery offering a menu of creative sushi rolls, Asian entrees and sake cocktails.
Favorites: Chicken Shu Mai, Fried Pork Dumplings and Coconut Green Curry Shrimp.

DETENTE RESTAURANT AND WINE BAR
15 Winter St, Edgartown, 508-627-8810
www.detentemv.com
CUISINE: New American
DRINKS: Full bar
SERVING: Dinner
PRICE RANGE: $$$
Modern, sophisticated seasonal kitchen offering a menu of fresh local products. Plates are very professional and stylishly prepared. Gorgeous. Small

portions. Not the place to come if you're starving.
Favorites: Lobster Ravioli and Hand rolled pastas.
Extensive wine list. Nice romantic patio out back in-
season.

ESPRESSO LOVE
17 Church St (behind the courthouse), Edgartown,
508-627-9211
www.espressolove.com
CUISINE: Coffee shops; Sandwiches & Salads
DRINKS: No booze
SERVING: Breakfast (from 6), lunch till 6 p.m.
PRICE RANGE: $
Great selection of fresh baked goods, good breakfast
items, hearty sandwiches and entrée sized salads for
lunch. But the COFFEE is a big attraction here, too.
Lots of celebs show up here. But there's room for
you, too. Very friendly. Christina Thornton (chef-
owner of **Hooked**), starts her morning here with an
iced coffee.

GIORDANO'S CLAM BAR
18 Lake Ave, Oak Bluffs, 508-693-0184
www.giosmv.com
CUISINE: Pizza
DRINKS: Full Bar
SERVING: Lunch, Dinner
PRICE RANGE: $$
Open for over 80 years, this place is known for its
family style Italian classics and pizza. (The whole
fried clams are a standout.) Carry-out window offers
a take-away option for those looking for a quick
lunch.

GRACE EPISCOPAL CHURCH LOBSTER ROLLS (Fridays Only)

36 Woodlawn Ave, Vineyard Haven, 508 693-0332
www.graceepiscopalmv.org/
CUISINE: Lobster Rolls
DRINKS: No Booze
SERVING: Dinner – seasonal hours
PRICE RANGE: $

It's hard to find a real bargain on expensive Cape Cod, but here's one. A Stuffed Lobster roll dinner for a very cheap price here at Grace. It's Fridays only (4 – 7:30), and runs in the summer, usually through the end of September. You get the lobster roll, chips, a drink, sometimes even dessert, when they have it. Other foods served – hot dogs and dessert. Eat in the rec hall or take it to go. Funds go to island nonprofits. Arrive early. The secret is out on this place, LOL.

LARSEN'S FISH MARKET
56 Basin Rd, Chilmark, 508-645-2680
www.larsensfishmarket.com
CUISINE: American
DRINKS: No Booze
SERVING: Breakfast (from 9), lunch & early dinner (till 7)
PRICE RANGE: $
In the fishing village of Menemsha. It is a great spot for clams or oysters on the half shell and to watch the sunset. (**Menemsha Beach** is one of the few places you can watch the sun set into the water.) Though the

big deal here is the fresh fish for sale in the market, their kitchen will cook to order these items: Lobster, Chowder of the Day, Lobster Bisque, Stuffed Quahogs, Stuffed Scallops, Crab Cakes, Steamers, Mussels. The seafood here is about an unadorned, unfancy and GOOD as you can get.

LITTLE HOUSE CAFÉ
339 State Rd, Vineyard Haven, 508-687-9794
www.littlehousemv.com
CUISINE: Mediterranean/American (Traditional)
DRINKS: Full bar
SERVING: B'fast, Lunch, & Dinner, Closed Sundays; this place closes for an hour between b'fast & lunch (11-11:30) and lunch & dinner (4 to 5), just so you know.

PRICE RANGE: $$
Cozy little café (just simple wooden chairs & tables, nothing fancy) serving international and American cuisine to a host of locals as well as the tourist who know enough to come here. Gluten-free and vegetarian options. Favorites: Fish tacos, curried mango chicken salad sandwich and Nonna's meatballs. Desserts are all homemade.

MENEMSHA FISH MARKET
54 Basin Rd, Chilmark, 508-645-2282
http://www.menemshafishmarket.com/
CUISINE: Seafood Market
DRINKS: Full bar
SERVING: 10 a.m. – 5 p.m.
PRICE RANGE: $$
Seafood market selling fresh seafood – local and international. Menu mainly features fresh seafood

dishes coming from their own market, everything from lobsters to red snapper, little necks, scallops and clam chowder. Good soups, sandwiches. Eat outside on the dock overlooking the fishing boats. Delivery available.

PORT HUNTER
55 Main St, Edgartown, 508-627-7747
www.theporthunter.com
CUISINE: Seafood
DRINKS: Full Bar
SERVING: Dinner
PRICE RANGE: $$S
Very friendly eatery that's so relaxed they offer tables for standing and regular seating. The décor matches the seafood-focused menu. Menu favorites include Quinoa fritters, fish tacos, Chatham mussels in a spicy curry sauce, Buffalo Brussels sprouts served

with a blue cheese mousse. Music later. Great cocktails and shuffleboard.

RED CAT KITCHEN
14 Kennebec Ave, Oak Bluffs, 508-696-6040
www.redcatkitchen.com
CUISINE: American (New)/Seafood
DRINKS: Full Bar
SERVING: Dinner
PRICE RANGE: $$$
A very welcoming atmosphere greets you here, whether you eat inside where you can enjoy art created by locals or outside on the porch beneath the Chinese lanterns. This place offers a very creative menu with names to match. Try the Island Fresca – a Parmesan soup with island corn, tomatoes, and basil that is quite famous locally. The dishes come with a great medley of local vegetables that makes every dish special.

SCOTTISH BAKEHOUSE
977 State Rd, Vineyard Haven, 508-693-6633
www.scottishbakehousemv.com
CUISINE: American
DRINKS: No Booze
SERVING: Breakfast, lunch, dinner
PRICE RANGE: $$
More to this place than meets the eye. Look at the
garden out back—a lot of the food they serve here
comes from it. Egg sandwich for b'fast is only $4;
full line of sandwiches for lunch, hefty wraps; entrees
include quesadilla; spicy peanut noodles; Brazilian
plate; kale & sweet potato mash; soups, salads, all
fresh, fresh, fresh. (They go through 100 pounds of
kale every week in season.) Specialty menu items for
you if you're vegan, a carnivore, localvore,
baconitarian, gluten free, sugar-free, you name it.
Open year round.

STATE ROAD
688 State Rd, West Tisbury, 508-693-8582
www.stateroadmv.com
CUISINE: Diners

DRINKS: No Booze
SERVING: Breakfast, lunch, dinner
PRICE RANGE: $$$
The Obamas liked this place, and so will you. Try the bacon cheddar Jalapeno grits for breakfast. (Hot!) Or the hash that changes daily. Lunch from 11 till 2: sandwiches and salads. Dinner (from 5:30) offers treats like sugar snap pea salad, shrimp & grits and lobster salad for starters, and items like loin of rabbit, lamb chops or prosciutto wrapped monkfish for main courses. Very nice spot. They have gardens out back that supply lots of the ingredients served here. This is a relatively new place on the Vineyard, but it still has a "tavern" feel to it, with wood beams and rustic chandeliers giving off a cozy glow.

THE SWEET LIFE CAFE
63 Circuit Ave, Oak Bluffs, 508-696-0200
www.sweetlifemv.com
CUISINE: American

DRINKS: Full Bar
SERVING: Dinner
PRICE RANGE: $$$$
Elegant spot with prices to match in this Victorian house offering up a romantic setting you'll love the minute you walk in. Great tuna tartare and very creative soups. The meats are top quality: lamb sirloin, breaded quail breast, dry-rubbed rib eye. (You can get seafood a hundred other places, right?) Has one of the better wine lists on the island.

Chapter 5
WHERE TO SHOP
(& SERVICES)

ALLEN WHITING GALLERY
985 State Rd, West Tisbury, 508-693-4691
allenwhiting.com
Gallery exhibiting the work of local artist Allen
Whiting – known for his oil paintings featuring
locales in the surrounding area.

ALLEY'S GENERAL STORE
1045 State Rd, West Tisbury, 508-693-0088
www.mvpreservation.org/properties/alleys-general-store/
This wonderful place has a sign out front that says, "Dealers in Almost Everything," and it's been here since 1858. It's always been a general store, so it's the kind of place where you get everything you need, kind of like an old fashioned 7-11 or convenience store. Must stop if you're in West Tisbury.

BESPOKE ABODE
56 Main St, Vineyard Haven, 508-687-9555
www.bespokeabode.com
This comfortable shop has lots of items for the home, especially if you're looking for that island feel.

Interior designer Liz Stiving-Nichols chooses everything: unusual picture frames, mirrors, pillows, some furniture.

CHICKEN ALLEY
38 Lagoon Pond Rd, Vineyard Haven, 508-693-2278.
www.chickenalley.org/
Unique thrift shop that is also part art gallery. A favorite of anybody who likes funky clothing. Shelves of used books, clothing, household items, furniture, artwork and collectibles. The shop hosts the annual Chicken Alley Art's and Collectible Sale on the 2nd Sunday in August.

THE CHILMARK COFFEE COMPANY
12 Lagemann Ln, Chilmark, 508-560-1061
chilmarkcoffeeco.com
Todd Christy has dedicated himself to creating the best coffee in the region and his coffees are sold all over the island. This is where it all starts.

CHILMARK GENERAL STORE
7 State Rd, Chilmark, 508-645-3739
www.chilmarkgeneralstore.com
An old-fashioned market is a locals' meeting place
and a great stop for lunch. The market sells island-
grown produce, coffee, household necessities, and
almost anything that you might need. Great
sandwiches and fresh organic coffee. Grab a slice of
their famous pizza and eat it on the porch.

FIELD GALLERY
1050 State Rd, West Tisbury, 508-693-5595
www.fieldgallery.com
This gallery has been exhibiting the work of island
artists for over 35 years and continues to feature a
group of talented artists. Rotating exhibitions of
contemporary paintings, sculpture, photography, and
other works. Artists' receptions are held Sunday
afternoons throughout the summer.

GRANARY GALLERY
636 Old Country Rd, West Tisbury, 508-693-0455
www.granarygallery.com
Not your typical gallery geared to tourists featuring
"island-y" paintings by local artists. This place
features high-end art, with the price tags to match—
sculpture, photos, and paintings—by some 70+ big
name international artists. (A few locals are
represented as well.) Owners are the discerning
Christopher and Sheila Morse.

MARTHA'S VINEYARD GLASSWORKS
683 State Rd, West Tisbury, 508-693-6026
www.mvglassworks.com
The glass works of 6 or 7 artists are on sale here in
this fine shop, from platters to bowls, tableware, jars,
vases, display pieces. Here you'll find any number of
inventive pieces that will make a great addition to
your home (or even your office) or as a gift.

MERMAID FARM & DAIRY
9 Middle Rd, Chilmark, 508-645-3492
www.facebook.com/Mermaid-Farm-and-Dairy-
371138872899/
Founded in 1997, this 35-acre farm and dairy sells a
variety of vegetables, raw milk, handmade yogurt,
feta cheese, wheat and rye flours, beef, lamb and
pork. Worth a visit.

NORTH TABOR FARM

4 North Tabor Farm Rd, Chilmark, 508-645-3311.
www.northtaborfarm.com/
A six-acre farm run by Rebecca Miller with a farm stand on premises selling fresh items like salad greens, eggs, pork, poultry, mushrooms, honey, and flowers.

TEA LANE FARM

161 Middle Rd, Chilmark, 774-563-8274
tealanefarm.com
Historic farm owned by the town of Chilmark. Krishana Collins sells her gorgeous flowers at the local farmers' market. Her services are available for weddings, special events, and flower services. The beautiful farm is ideal for hiking, mountain biking and dog walking.

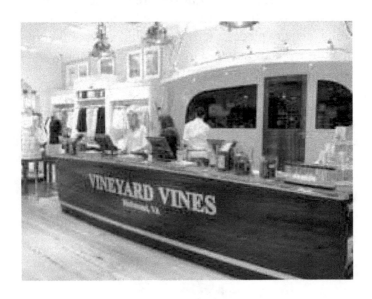

VINEYARD VINES

27 N Water St, Edgartown, 508-627-4779
www.vineyardvines.com
Great books, gifts, polo shirts, lots of gifts focusing
on the Vineyard.

WEST TISBURY FARMERS MARKET

1067 State Road, West Tisbury, 508-693-5161
www.wtfmarket.org
Runs from Jun – Oct, Wed & Sat, 9 – noon, rain or
shine. The fruits and vegetables you can buy here
come from people on the Vineyard who grew them.
Lots of fun. (They also have an abbreviated winter
market.) Questions? Contact Linda Alley at 508-693-
9561, or email linda@newlanesundries.com

Chapter 6
WHAT TO SEE & DO

AQUINNAH BEACH
MOSHUP BEACH / NUDE BEACH
www.mvy.com
On the west side of the island is this nice public beach
with some parking. Here you'll get to see the cliffs of
clay, which rise straight up from the long stretch of
lonely beach. (Plan on walking.) The nude section of
the beach is at the north end.

THE CAMPGROUND

Oak Bluffs, 508-693-0525

www.mvcma.org

Email: office@mvcma.org

Here they have an organization called the Martha's
Vineyard Camp Meeting Association (MVCMA), that
is quite interesting and well worth your time to
investigate. They have numerous activities and events
in the summer season. There are dozens of Victorian
gingerbread cottages. While the cottages were
ostensibly built by devout Methodists who set up
"camps" when they met here, beginning as far back as
1835, there's been a lot of restoration. Once a year
they do a Grand Illumination (I know, it sounds like
something from another world) when they hang
colorful Japanese and Chinese lanterns in all the
cottages. (Usually in the middle of August.) Fun place
for the whole family.

CEDAR TREE NECK SANCTUARY

Vineyard Haven

www.sheriffsmeadow.org

Here you will find a lovely, preserved area that offers
splendid, relaxed views of forestry, a pond and the
ocean beyond. Cedar Creek is maintained by the
Sheriff's Meadow Foundation, which has an
interesting history. Over in Edgartown, Sheriff Isaiah
Pease owned a meadow that came to be known as
Sheriff's Meadow. On it there was a pond used in the
winter to cut ice for storage later in the year. Henry
Beetle Hough, the editor of the local "Vineyard
Gazette," lived nearby and his windows looked out
onto the meadow. When he heard the area was going

to be developed, he used $7,000, the advance for a book from a New York publisher, to buy the meadow and preserve it. When none of the other preservation groups wanted to take the property, he and wife Elizabeth launched the Sheriff's Meadow Foundation, which now boasts many other areas of Martha's Vineyard that will be preserved for years to come.

CHAPPAQUIDDICK
You can jump on a ferry to Chappaquiddick, which is only 300 yards off the Vineyard's east coast. Here you can enjoy miles of empty beaches (depending on the time of year and day you go). Bird watchers flock here to look at spot blue herons, sandpipers and the like.

DR. DANIEL FISHER HOUSE
99 Main St, Edgartown, 508-627-4440
https://vineyardtrust.org/
Built in 1840, this Federal style residence is open for visitors and available for weddings and such.

EDGARTOWN LIGHTHOUSE
In Edgartown Harbor
www.mvmuseum.org/edgartown.php
In front of the **Harbor View Hotel**, take the path off N Water St.

FISHING WITH JENNIFER CLARKE
Chilmark, 508-776-7286
captainclarkecharters.com
Jennifer Clarke, also a successful singer/songwriter, offers a wide variety of charter fishing excursions.

Climb aboard Captain Clarke's 30-foot center console
charter vessel "Femme Fatale" for what I promise you
will be a memorable experience. Martha's Vineyard
is a fisherman's paradise boasting the best in striped
bass, bluefish, bonito, false albacore, fluke and sea
bass fishing.

FLYING HORSES CAROUSEL
15 Oak Bluffs Ave, Oak Bluffs, 508-693-9481
www.mvpreservation.org
Open from Easter Sunday through Columbus Day.
This is one of the oldest carousels in America and a
national landmark, and you just must see it, even if
you don't take a ride. Its horses were hand-carved in
1876 in New York City, one of 2 known carousels
built by Charles W. F. Dare. In 1884, the Flying
Horses were brought from Coney Island to Martha's
Vineyard and have been operating on the same site
for more than a century. Rides are cheap. (And if you
catch the brass ring you can get a free ride.)

GAY HEAD LIGHTHOUSE
15 Aquinnah Circle, Aquinnah, 508-645-9954/508-645-2300
Tues-Sat, mid-June through mid-Sept.
www.gayheadlight.org

GREAT ROCK BIGHT PRESERVE
37 Brickyard Rd, Chilmark, 508-627-7141
mvlandbank.com
Owned by the Martha's Vineyard Land bank, this preserve is free to visit. The preserve features many trails and access to 1,300 feet of beach along the Vineyard Sound. The preserve is used for nature study, hiking, picnicking, mountain-biking, horseback

riding, hunting (with permission), fishing, and swimming.

ISLAND ALPACA
1 Head of Pond Rd, Vineyard Haven, 508-693-5554
www.islandalpaca.com
They breed alpacas here on this 20-acre farm. You can feed the critters and take them for walks. But you'll want to visit the gift store with its clothes for babies, footwear, handbags, totes, purses, jackets, coats, hats, headbands sweaters, scarves, shawls—all made of alpaca here on Martha's Vineyard.

JAWS BRIDGE
Seaview Ave, Edgartown
If you want to see what MV looked like in 1975 (and see what's changed and how much hasn't), take a look at Steven Spielberg's 1975 film, "Jaws."
The film crew descended on Edgartown with their 24-foot shark and took the place over for a few months. You'll see lots of houses, stores and other locations in the movie that are still here.

Jaws Bridge is officially the **American Legion Memorial Bridge**, but locals refer to it as **Big Bridge**. It's part of Seaview Avenue, which connects Edgartown with the town of Oak Bluffs. The bridge also divides the Atlantic Ocean from Sengekontacket Pond.

Despite its nickname, the bridge is a small one, just a few car-lengths in total, and it has been refurbished in recent years. The stone quay Roy Scheider ran during the Jaws attack at the bridge is still there and runs perpendicular to the bridge. The beach on the ocean side, called Joseph Sylvia State Beach, was where the rest of the scene was filmed.

LIGHTHOUSE BEACH
Water St, Edgartown, 508-627-6145
No Website
You can get spectacular views of Chappaquiddick from the top of this 45-foot-high cast iron lighthouse after climbing the spiral staircase. Originally built in

1881 and installed at Ipswich, Mass., it was taken apart and brought here after the lighthouse in Edgartown was damaged in a hurricane.

LONG POINT WILDLIFE REFUGE
Hughe's Thumb Rd, 508-693-3678
Off the Edgartown – West Tisbury Road
www.thetrustees.org/places-to-visit/cape-cod-islands/long-point.html
Salt and freshwater ponds, hundreds of acres of beautiful virgin beachfront. At more than 600 acres, Long Point is one of the largest publicly accessible properties on Martha's Vineyard. It encompasses beach, dune, and woodland that surround a broad (and uncommon) sand plain heath. While busy in season,

the refuge is especially fun in the winter.
(Birdwatchers love it.)

THE MARTHA'S VINEYARD MUSEUM
151 Lagoon Pond Rd, Vineyard Haven, 508-627-
4441
www.marthasvineyardhistory.org
Authoritative source for history and genealogy on the
island. Excellent exhibits including the Thomas
Cooke house, the Francis Foster Museum, the Captain
Francis Pease House and Carriage Shed with
coverage of whaling and Wampanoag history as well.
Modest admission.

OLD WHALING CHURCH
89 Main St, Edgartown, 508-627-4442
https://vineyardtrust.org/property/old-whaling-
church/
Built by whaling captains in 1843, this landmark is
considered on of the finest examples of Greek
Revival architecture in New England.

MENEMSHA BEACH
Basin Rd, Chilmark
Just a couple of minutes' walk from the fishing
village that gives this beach its name, you'll find
perhaps the BEST sunset on Martha's Vineyard.

VINCENT HOUSE MUSEUM
99 A Main St, Edgartown, 508-627-8017
https://vineyardtrust.org/property/vincent-house-
gardens/
Built in 1672, this is probably the oldest standing
house on Martha's Vineyard. The museum houses
furnishings that show examples of Puritan life to the
more elegant Whaling era.

Chapter 7
NIGHTLIFE

Nightlife options are somewhat limited by the nature of Martha's Vineyard. In addition, only 2 towns allow alcohol to be sold: Edgartown and Oak Bluffs. Vineyard Haven has jumped in and now lets restaurants serve beer and wine (but no hard liquor), and then you must have food served as well.

These are odd rules you expect in backwater counties in North Carolina, but not up here. Anyway, in the other towns, West Tisbury, Chilmark and Aquinnah, you must BYOB.

Some of these are really restaurants, but because they have a lively bar scene, I've put them here to "create" a nightlife" section.

OFFSHORE ALE CO
30 Kennebec Ave, Oak Bluffs, 508-693-2626
www.offshoreale.com
This locals' pub is also the only brewery on Martha's Vineyard, and as easily could be in the "What To See & Do" chapter. As such, it's better as a nightlife destination, there being so few places to go here on Martha's Vineyard at night. Toss those peanut shells right on the floor. They don't care. Get the Offshore Amber Ale that's made right there on the premises.

RITZ CAFÉ
4 Circuit Ave, Oak Bluffs, 508-693-9851
www.theritzmv.com
On the dock you'll find this dive bar that has live music nightly during season (but off season only on weekends).

SHARKY'S CANTINA
31 Circuit Ave, Oak Bluffs, 508-693-7501
266 Upper Main St, Edgartown, 508-627-6565
www.sharkyscantina.com
They boast "50 menu items under $10," so this is a good place to bring the kids. But the bar is busy at night.

INDEX

NOTES

NOTES

NOTES